LLC Beginner's Guide

Lucas Edholm

Everything You Need to Know to Start, Run, and Grow Your Limited Liability Company

A FREE GIFT TO OUR READERS

Enter your email below to get your bonus ebooks and checklists!

1. LLC Formation Checklist
2. LLC Marketing Checklist
3. The Productivity Secrets of Successful Entrepreneurs (ebook)
4. 32 Sales Closing Techniques (ebook)

Get it here:

Table of Contents

What is an LLC?

An LLC, (Limited Liability Company) is the most popular type of business structure. The first US-based LLC was created in Wyoming in 1977. By the year 1996, LLC statutes had been established in all 50 states. The basic idea was to allow business owners to create a tax-friendly company while maintaining a level of protection for their personal assets.

Because of its flexibility and simplicity, the popularity of the LLC business structure has grown exponentially. Today, there are over 21 million LLCs in the United States compared to approximately 1.7 million traditional C-Corporations.

Let's assume that you are a small business owner or an entrepreneur. Then you have several choices to give a legal structure to your activity: sole proprietorships, general partnerships, corporations, LLC, etc. The structure you choose for your business will determine who owns the business, how taxes are paid, and who is liable in case of a lawsuit or debts. In most cases, starting an LLC is the simplest and most effective way to protect your assets, establish credibility, and save on your taxes.

Let us consider some of the main reasons for which it may be worth opening an LLC.

An LLC is its own legal entity, separate from its owners. This creates what is known as a 'corporate veil' between you as a person and the activities of your business. Having an LLC keeps the owner's personal assets secure in the event of a lawsuit or unpaid business debt.

Being a legal entity means that the LLC as a corporation has its own legal responsibilities (which include tax filing) as well as legal rights. For instance, it can enter into contracts either as a vendor or a supplier and can sue or be sued in a court of law.

LLCs have pass-through taxation. That is, you are not taxed at the entity level. When a corporation makes a profit, that profit is taxed, distributed to the owners, and then taxed again as personal income. An LLC's profits are not taxed. The income passes straight to the business owner who only pays personal income taxes for their share of the business.

For LLCs there are no strict requirements for record keeping. Business accounting and compliance can be complicated and confusing, especially for a beginner entrepreneur.
LLCs, compared to other corporate structures, simplify the formation and keeping of business records, making them easy to maintain even for single-owner businesses.

In summary, an LLC allows you to protect your assets, pay fewer taxes and reduce paperwork. But that is not all. There are many other reasons why you might want to start your LLC, including privacy or the fact that owners of an LLC need not be US citizens or permanent residents. We will look more in-depth at the advantages and possibilities offered by LLCslater in the book. But first, let's take a look at the different types of LLCs.

Different Types of LLCs

As if choosing a business structure was not enough, you also have to choose among different types of LLCs. But don't worry. If you have a clear goal in mind, it will be easy to pick the type of LLC that is most suitable for your business.

Single-Member LLC (SMLLC)

The name is self-explanatory. A single-member limited liability company has only one owner or member. That individual bears the full responsibility of the company, including being accountable for tax payments.

This is by far the most popular form of LLC used by beginner entrepreneurs or freelancers. They start out with a single-member LLC and still enjoy the freedom of adding partners to their business at a later time.

Having the option of incorporating more partners can be essential when raising funds and trying to grow your company. At that stage, you might want to transition to a Multi-Member LLC.

Multi-Member LLC (MMLLC)

Once again, the name is self-explanatory. An MMLLC has multiple owners. These can be individuals, other LLCs, or corporations.

Although technically, an MMLC can have an arbitrary number of members, the most popular type is a two-member LLCfor businesses run by a husband/wife couple or by two friends who act as partners.

The most important difference between an SMLLC and an MMLLC concerns the way in which taxes are paid.

The IRS treats an SMLLC as a "disregarded entity." That is, **the income generated by the LLC is reported on the owner's personal federal tax return.** In other words, no separate federal tax return is necessary for the SMLLC. This process is called "pass-through taxation." The sole owner of the LLC is personally responsible for paying the taxes for the income generated by the business.

Multi-member LLCs, instead, are treated by the IRS as partnerships. **A multiple-member LLC must file a tax return** and give its members K-1 forms to file with their returns. Unsurprisingly, having more members means more paperwork.

There is another aspect in which a single-member LLC differs from a multi-member one. While it is highly recommended to have an operating agreement in both cases, as we will see more in detail later, in the case of a multiple-member company, the drafting of this document requires a much higher degree of attention.

You must make sure that the rights of each member are clearly spelled out, especially in the case of events that will break the partnership, such as the death of one of the members or an irreconcilable disagreement. Prevention is better than cure.

SMLLC or MMLLC?

It seems like an easy choice, and most of the time, it is. If you are alone in your business, then you should probably go for an SMLLC, while if you have one or more business partners, then your best option is likely an MMLC. However, you should keep an open mind and **consider the advantages and disadvantages of both options.**

There are cases in which it is convenient for a single business owner to form a multiple-member company. For instance, they might want to add their spouse or parents as members to gain further asset protection. On the other hand, there are situations in which it is convenient for two or more people in a partnership to start single-member companies. This often happens in real estate investing.

Consider the following example. Alice and Bob are in a 50% partnership and bought ten properties as separate LLCs. To simplify their taxes, they made all these SMLLCs owned by an MMLLC, of which they are both members. With this strategy, they avoid having to file a separate tax return for each property.

Remember that **a single-member LLC is easier to manage for tax purposes because, as a "disregarded entity," no federal tax return is required.**

The example in the previous paragraph introduces us to another important distinction, which is the one between holding LLCs and operating LLCs.

Holding LLC

A holding LLC is a company that exists only to hold assets, like real estate, or to act as an umbrella holding company for other subsidiary companies. In the example of Alice and Bob, they have ten operating LLCs and one holding LLC.
Holding companies are created to have additional layers of protection and, in some cases, as in the example above, to simplify taxes. Your first LLC will surely be an operating company, but as your business grows, keep in mind the option of instituting this further level of protection from liability.

Member-Managed LLC vs. Manager-Managed LLC

A Member-Managed LLC is one where one of the owners runs the daily operations of the company. This is the usual structure and the one that most likely applies to you. The other option is a Manager-Managed LLC, where the operations of the company are run by someone different than the owners.

Domestic LLC vs. Foreign LLC

What is a Foreign LLC? Despite the name, it doesn't mean that the company comes from another country. Instead, it means your business was organized under the laws of a different state. **An LLC is domestic in the state where it is created and foreign everywhere else.**

When you conduct business outside of the state in which the LLC was created, you are required to register your company as a Foreign LLC (you must obtain the so-called "foreign qualification"). Registration is used to make sure that your company meets the regulations and tax requirements of the foreign state.

A company needs to acquire foreign qualifications when it grows and expands its business into other states. But it is also common for LLCs to be formed in states with business-friendly tax laws and operate as foreign companies in their home state.

One or many LLCs?

As we will see in the next chapters, opening and maintaining an LLC has certain costs. If you are involved in several businesses, you might be wondering whether it is worth opening a new LLC for each of your projects. The answer is not so straightforward and depends on your individual situation.

It is recommended to keep all your activities under the same LLC if the following circumstances apply:

- You have the same ownership structure in all your businesses. For instance, if all are solo projects.
- Your projects are relatively low risk, so you are not taking on debt.
- You are not likely to get sued, and therefore you are not worried about the liabilities issues of the projects to each other.
- Many of your projects are experimental, that is, new ideas that you are just testing out. In this case, it is better to keep the business structure lean and simple by operating all your activities under the same LLC.

You should create a different LLC for each business if you find yourself in the following circumstances.

- The ownership structure is different for each business. For instance, one project is solo, and another is in partnership.
- One (or more) of the businesses is high risk. If one project is taking a lot of debt, has lots of employees, or might be involved in litigation, then it is appropriate to keep it separate from your other businesses.
- If you are developing a branch of your business with the purpose of selling it, then it would be better to have it under a separate entity.

In any case, it is always wise to investigate possible tax benefits coming from separating your business activities into different LLCs.

Advantages and Disadvantages of an LLC

What are the Advantages of an LLC?

Business owners have plenty of advantages when they register their business as an LLC:

- **You only have limited liability.** As an owner, you are not personally responsible for the debts or liabilities of the business. When an LLC is set up properly, the assets of the owners are not used to pay off business debts. LLCassets, on the other hand, are used to wipe out debts.
- **Pass-through taxation.** Usually, the LLC is not taxed at the business level. The owner reports the income or loss of the LLC on his/her personal federal tax return. Therefore, it is the business owner who pays any due taxes.
- **Flexible distribution of losses and profits among owners.** Owners have flexibility in distributing losses and profits among the owners of the LLC.
- **No restrictions regarding the ownership of the LLC.** An LLC does not have a limit of fifty owners as an S corporation does. At most, there are very few ownership restrictions, but typically there are none.

- **No strictness regarding management.** LLC owners have a free hand in structuring the management of the company.
- **Various classes of membership.** Unlike in S corporations, where there is only one class of membership, for LLCs, there are various membership classes available. These are established in the Operating Agreement of the company.
- **Less bureaucracy.** LLCs have less yearly paperwork than C corporations and S corporations. They also do not have to comply with meeting requirements imposed on C and S corporations.
- **Trustworthiness.** Registering your company as an LLC may help increase the trustworthiness of your business. Typically an LLC is perceived as more legitimate than a business registered as a general partnership or a sole proprietorship.
- **Consent in written form is required to add new owners or increase the ownership of an LLC.** The consent must be provided before ownership is given to others.

What Are the Disadvantages of an LLC?

It is not completely risk-free. Although an LLC is responsible and assumes all the risk if the company is sued, you still risk losing your business. For instance, if you run an interior design company and damage your client's property or injure your client, she can sue your company.

- **It costs more to set up.** Registering a company as an LLC requires more legal paperwork, and you incur more costs than if you choose to register it as a sole proprietorship. Some of these costs include expenses for the paperwork you need to file with the state and the formation fee. Typically you can get a free business Employer Identification Number (EID), but you still have to fill out the paperwork and apply.

- **An LLC might not be worthwhile for your business.** In certain cases, businesses do not earn enough or might not make enough profits for the tax benefits of operating an LLC to outweigh the costs.

- **You pay taxes on all profits.** An LLC is a pass-through entity. That is, you personally get the profits and pay taxes on your business at your personal tax rate. You benefit because the personal tax rate is lower than the C or S corporation tax rate. However, you are taxed on all of your profits, i.e., even if you want to keep money in your business for further investments in your company. Said otherwise, you will be unable to make tax-deductible investments in your business. (There are some exceptions related to the set-up costs of your LLC). It is recommended to hire a tax advisor to find out whether an LLC makes sense for you in this case.

- **Profits are subject to Social Security taxes.** In certain cases, the owners of an LLC could end up paying more in taxes than those of a corporation since both salaries and profits are subject to self-employment taxes. They currently amount to 15.3% – 12.4% for Social Security and 2.9% for Medicare. When a company is registered as a corporation, only salaries are subject to taxation.

- **Profits must be recognized straight away.** LLCs are not subject to double taxation. This means that the profits generated by an LLC are reported automatically in the members' income. In contrast, C-corporations do not have to distribute profits to shareholders straight away. Therefore, shareholders do not always have to pay taxes on the profits of the corporation.

- **Fringe benefits and taxable income.** The fringe benefits received by the employees of an LLC, such as medical insurance or parking, must be treated as taxable income. In contrast, C-corporation employees who also receive fringe benefits do not have to pay income taxes on the benefits they receive.

Is an LLC Right for You?

Choosing your business structure can be one of the most intimidating steps of your business. You have already found a market, you have an idea, and your clients are ready to pay for your product or service. You now find yourself researching the different business structures and wondering which one is the best choice for your business. Is it better to keep it simple and be a sole proprietor, or should you have a corporation? Should you choose the middle ground and opt for an LLCinstead?

Many different structures exist to meet the needs of various types of businesses. For instance, an S-Corporation has a board of directors and shareholders. They must hold annual meetings and record minutes. An LLC, on the other hand, does not have the same formal requirements. This is one of the reasons why an LLC is a good fit for many small to medium-sized businesses. It allows business owners to form a legitimate business (with liability protections) without many of the formal requirements necessary for a corporation.

When deciding whether to form an LLC or some other entity, business owners look at the benefits and risks of each structure and weigh them against the needs of their business. Next, they choose the structure that best fits their business needs.

Here are some questions you should ask yourself to decide if an LLC is the right choice for you:

Am I working by myself or with others?

Regardless if you start a business with your best friend from childhood or with an acquaintance you met at a dinner, partnering with someone entails a lot of risks. The effort it takes to register your business as an LLC pales in comparison to the potential negative consequences you may have to face if your partnership goes downhill. When you opt for an LLC, you ensure that the LLC - not you - will be liable in case your business partner makes a bad decision.

Will I be at risk of getting sued?

Did you know that between 36% and 53% of all small businesses get sued every year and that a whopping 43% are threatened with lawsuits? Moreover, 90% of all businesses are sued at least one time during their lifespan. As you can see from these numbers, business owners are far more likely than private persons to be sued, and this is not surprising at all. There are certain risks that come with providing a service or selling a product. Your clients might be dissatisfied with the product, delayed delivery might have negative repercussions, and unexpected events might displease some of your customers in an irreconcilable way. Therefore, it is almost always better to form an LLC not to put your personal assets at risk.

If the risk of being sued is particularly high for your business, an LLC is the recommended choice. Here is how you can determine if you have a high-risk business:

- You have employees who are at risk of injuring themselves during working hours.
- Customers may suffer harm when using your product (e.g., cosmetic products).
- Your customers could claim that you provided a service that was below the professional standard of care (e.g., medical malpractice).
- You work with suppliers or consumers who might sue you for breaching a contract.
- Your employees could file a lawsuit for discrimination or unjustified termination.

Note: Some states will not allow you to form an LLC if you are a licensed professional. Therefore, you might want to consider forming a corporation or a professional limited liability company instead.

Is this a side gig?

Is this a small, low-risk business that you work on besides your job? Is your goal just to make a little money on the side? Then an LLC might not be the most suitable structure for you.

The amount of effort it takes to form an LLC is just not worth it for such a small business, especially if the LLC fees in your state are so high that they significantly diminish your profit.

What are my future plans for my business?

One of the factors that you should take into consideration when choosing your business structure is the future of your company. An LLC reduces the liability of the owner and offers protection similar to a corporation. Nevertheless, there are certain cases in which you might need a corporation instead of an LLC. For instance, the owners of a corporation own shares of stocks in their business. On the other hand, LLC owners own equity in the assets of their business.

If you plan to sell shares of stocks in your business in the future, the prerequisite is that your business is registered as a corporation. Therefore, it is important to consider how you envision the future of your business when deciding whether to create an LLC.

Should You Create an LLC Holding Company?

What Is a Holding Company?

A holding company, or umbrella company, is a parent business entity, that is, a corporation with subsidiaries. These subsidiaries are separate businesses that are wholly or partially owned by the parent. The holding company itself does not conduct any standard business operations, which are left to the subsidiaries. Specifically, the holding company does not manufacture any products, nor does it sell any products or services. As the name suggests, the holding company only holds stocks or other forms of ownership in the child companies (subsidiaries).

While a holding company does not conduct business operations on its own, it owns other companies that may sell services and products or manufacture goods. It may also hold other assets such as real estate properties or real estate portfolios, vehicles, equipment, or anything else that can be of value to the operations of the subsidiaries of the holding company.

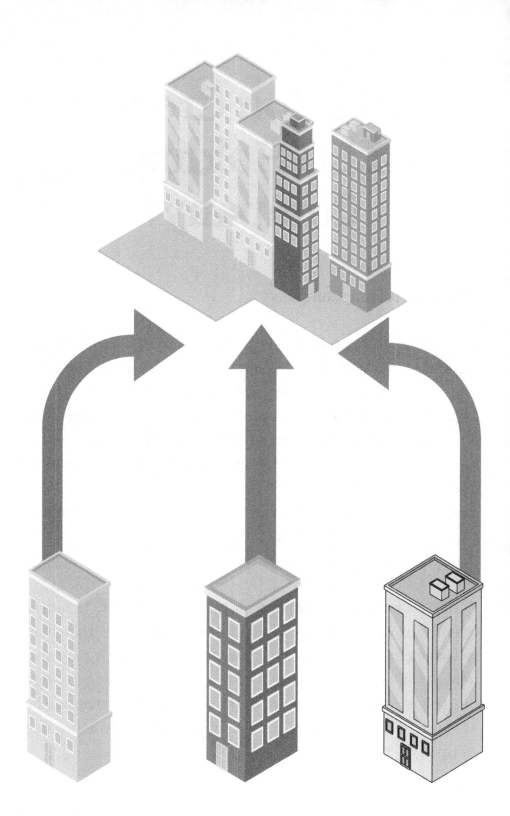

One of the most famous holding companies is Warren Buffett's Berkshire Hathaway. The company owns and controls many different businesses, such as GEICO and Dairy Queen.

A holding company may own 100% of a subsidiary, or it can simply have enough interest to maintain control through voting rights. This usually means any share of ownership that is above 51%. Having this sort of control gives the holding company the power to run and oversee the activities of the child companies. For instance, the management team of an LLC holding company can elect or remove directors or managers. They can also make major policy decisions, such as merging or even dissolving a subsidiary. However, each child company has its own management who runs the day-to-day operations. The management of each child company can make decisions about internal operations such as hiring, firing, and how to operate more effectively and efficiently. The people running the holding company do not participate in the managing of the business operations of their subsidiaries.

How Can an LLC Holding Company Be Financed?

The people who run the holding company are responsible for deciding where to invest its money. They have to constantly ask themselves questions such as "Should we buy more real estate?", "Should we buy a manufacturing plant?" or "What other assets would be valuable to our holding company?".

Holding companies usually have three different ways to raise money:

1. Selling equity or interest in the holding company. This means that the company will be recruiting other people interested in having stocks in the holding company or in any of its subsidiaries.
2. Borrowing money from other investors or banks.
3. Reinvesting its profits from the subsidiaries, such as dividends, distributions, or rent payments. Raising money as an LLC holding company tends to be easier than for an operating LLC because there are more members involved, and the company itself owns more assets.

How Can a Holding Company Be Used?

A holding company can be used by any type of business regardless of size or industry. Therefore, small businesses or even single-member entrepreneurs can start a holding company.

Let us consider the following example. Imagine that you want to buy an apartment as a real estate investment. You should consider the option of forming two LLCs. One LLC would own the apartment building, and the other LLC would be the holding company. If later on you want to expand your investment, you can raise money by selling shares in your existing holding company.

Together, you would own two businesses. One would be the apartment building investment, and the other the e-commerce store.

Here comes the interesting part. When you have a holding company with multiple assets that drive revenue and profitability, then you can position your holding company for a major buyout. You could sell your holding company for millions of dollars to large investment firms or venture capitalists who are keen on closing big deals. In fact, many publicly traded companies on the stock market are holding companies that constantly try to improve their revenues and increase the price per share of their stocks. Interestingly enough, many people who buy stocks don't even realize that they are investing in a holding company and not the actual operating company.

The main point to keep in mind is that holding companies are more ubiquitous than one might think. Small holding companies have a greater chance (than operating companies) of being acquired by larger holding companies.

Advantages of an Umbrella Company

Liability protection. By having a parent LLC (the holding company) and multiple child LLCs (the subsidiaries), you have complete separation of each entity. This provides powerful liability protection between each entity because the debts of each subsidiary belong solely to that subsidiary.

If we go back to the e-commerce example, imagine that your e-commerce store is struggling, and you are not able to pay off some of its debt. In that case, the creditor cannot go after the apartment building owned by the holding company. Creditors are only entitled to the assets that belong to the e-commerce store. Please note that it is important to be careful about the documents you sign. If you sign an agreement saying that you are personally liable for any debts or obligations, then your LLC cannot protect you against that.

Strong financing ability. Having an LLC holding company makes it easier for you to raise money. As mentioned before, you can raise money from other members of your holding company by selling interest in your companies or by seeking outside investment opportunities. Typically, a start-up or a new business is considered to be a great credit risk and may struggle with getting any type of investment. In contrast, when you have an established holding company, the investment is perceived as less risky. And it is not just a perception. If you obtain a loan with your holding company and then divert it to a start-up subsidiary, it is not only the start-up that is on the hook for that loan but the entire parent company.

Lower management needs. Each holding company will have its own management team to run the day-to-day operations. The holding company members simply make strategic investment decisions.

These types of decisions don't require as much time as managing a company's daily activities, thus giving the owners a lot more flexibility.

A holding company may foster innovation. When you have a business that is doing extremely well as an entrepreneur, you try to do your best to maintain that positive momentum. Investing in a new idea or a start-up within that business can be risky and bring the momentum down. In contrast, when you have a holding company, you can simply place your new business idea or your new start-up idea into its own separate entity without compromising the other. (Check out also the section titled One or many LLCs?) For instance, in 2015, Google restructured and formed the holding company Alphabet (of which Google became a subsidiary) because they wanted to invest in other ventures, such as Google Glasses or Youtube, without compromising their core business.

Disadvantages of an Umbrella Company

Costs. The more entities you have, the higher your set-up costs and annual fees. It can cost anywhere between USD 100 to USD 500 per year per each LLC that you own. Besides that, each entity would also need its own books, so you have separate bookkeeping expenses. For this, as well as to keep track of taxes, you would need to hire someone part-time or full-time, which means additional costs. Costs are usually the main factor deterring people from starting holding companies.

Management challenges. Remember that a holding company is not involved in the day-to-day operations, but they do help elect the directors and managers of a subsidiary. Can you see the issue with this? Imagine the following scenario. You know ten times more than what your boss knows about the running of your business, yet she or he is the one to elect the managers of your company. If the wrong people are running the holding company, then they can drive the subsidiaries **into failure.**

Complexity. Holding companies often have more compliance requirements and are governed by local, state, and federal laws. Even the way your taxes are done will be completely different when you have a holding company. Therefore, you also need to maintain important documents, records, assets, liabilities, and other properties completely separate from one another. This requires a skill of extreme organization. If you end up mixing any of your assets, books, or financialstogether, then any creditor that is after you may also go after your other business assets due to the lack of separation.

In conclusion, there are some great advantages of having a holding company, but if you aren't organized, or you don't hire help, you can find yourself with a huge headache trying to get everything sorted out.

To sum it up, just remember that an LLC holding company is a business entity that does not conduct business operations. Instead, it owns and controls other companies. Holding companies can help you grow your business and mitigate risks, but they can also be costly and complicated to manage.

How to Form an LLC?

How do you form an LLC?

A great option for small businesses and single-owners, LLCs are formal business structures recognized at the state and federal level that constitute a flexible and simple alternative to corporations. As we have already discussed, LLCs allow business owners to protect their personal assets, gain credibility, minimize taxes and streamline their administrative responsibilities.

Best of all, **they are easy and inexpensive to start.** There are two ways to start an LLC: You can form one yourself, or you can hire a service to do it for you. In this chapter, we will take a look at both options and help you decide how to go about forming your own Limited Liability Company.

Let's start by looking at how to form an LLC on your own, which requires a bit of work but can save you some money. The process does not require lots of complicated paperwork, and you can easily find all of the necessary forms online. Every state has different laws, and we recommend that you make yourself familiar with them depending on your preferred state.

Generally speaking, there are six steps you must take to start a new LLC.

Step One: Choose Your State

For most new business owners, the obvious option is to form an LLC in the state where you live and where you plan to conduct your business. When an LLC is first formed in a state, it is also known as a "Domestic LLC" in that state. If your business then expands to other states, your domestic LLC will need to be registered as a foreign LLC in every other state where you have a physical presence or employees. There are sometimes benefits to forming your LLC in a state with business-friendly laws, such as Delaware or Nevada. However, the tax advantages must be balanced against the extra fees and paperwork of having to register your LLC in multiple states.

Step Two: Choose a Name

Next, you will need to choose a name for your business. Every state has its own rules about what kind of names are allowed for LLCs. In general, you will need to observe these naming guidelines: Your name must include the phrase "limited liability company" or one of its abbreviations (LLC or L.L.C.). Restricted words such as Bank, Attorney, Law Office, etc., may require additional paperwork and may also need a licensed professional to be part of the LLC.

Your name cannot include words that could confuse your LLC with a government agency such as the FBI, Treasury, State Department, etc. You cannot use a name that has already been registered. To see if a name is available in your chosen state, you will need to perform a name search. You can do this for free on your state's Secretary of State website. We also recommend that you check to see if your business name is available as a web domain. Even if you don't plan to make a business website today, you may want to buy that URL in order to prevent others from acquiring it.

Step Three: Nominate a Registered Agent

At this point, you will need to nominate a registered agent for your LLC. Depending on your state, a registered agent is sometimes referred to as a resident agent, statutory agent, or agent for service of process. A registered agent is a person or business that acts as a point of contact for matters regarding your company. In fact, they send and receive legal papers on your behalf. Legal papers include any sort of official correspondence from legal summons to document filings. Your agent will receive these documents and then forward them to you. Your registered agent must be a resident of the state you're doing business in or a corporation authorized to conduct business in that state. If you nominate an individual, they can be a member of your LLC, including yourself. Most people, however, opt for using a registered agent company. Let's see why.

Technically, any person over 18 years old can be a registered agent, but there are some requirements that must be met:

- They must have a physical address (not just a post office box) in the state where your LLC is registered.
- They must be available in person during business hours at that address.

There might be some downsides to acting as your own registered agent. The first is privacy. Remember that the name and address of your registered agent are part of the public record. Therefore, if you are running your business from your house, you might not want to act as your own agent. Consider also that every time you move, you will have to promptly notify the state of your address change. Finally, remember that you must designate a registered agent in every state in which your company operates.

Step Four: File Formation Documents

To officially create an LLC, you will need to file formation documents with the secretary of state. The most common name for this document is "Articles of Organization." It is also known in some states as a "Certificate of Formation" or "Certificate of Organization." Your LLC formation document outlines the organizational structure of your business.

The Articles of Organization require three primary pieces of information:

One: Your LLC's unique and legal name.
Two: The name and street address of your registered agent.
Three: You must decide who will act as the manager of the LLC.

There are two options:
The first is Member-managed, where all members of the LLC manage the company. This is good for small organizations, where everyone is involved in day-to-day operations.

The second option is manager-managed, where individuals other than the owners are appointed to manage the LLC. This second model is appropriate for larger organizations, where not everyone is involved in the day-to-day affairs of the business.

At this stage, you will also have to pay a one-time processing fee to the secretary of state. This cost varies per state, but the price ranges between 40 and 500 dollars, with an average of about 125 dollars. Once you have filed your Articles of Organization and paid the fees, the state will then process your application. Most states process an application in three to seven working days. If the application is successful, you will have officially formed an LLC. The most common reason why an application is rejected is that the LLC naming guidelines were not followed.

Step Five: Create an Operating Agreement

Although not every state requires it, you should always create an operating agreement to establish ownership terms and member roles for your LLC. This foundational document is the core of your LLC and will help you maintain your organization, as well as further establish your LLC as a separate legal entity. There are six main sections of an operating agreement:

- **Organization.** This section outlines when and where the company was created, who the members are, and how ownership is structured.
- **Management and Voting.** This section addresses how the company is managed, as well as how the members vote.
- **Capital Contributions.** This part concerns the financial aspects of the company. It should contain information such as which members financially support the LLC and in which ways the company will raise further funds in the future.
- **Distributions.** This section must cover how the company's profits and losses will be shared among members.
- **Membership Changes.** This section describes the process for adding or removing members. Moreover, it details when and how members can transfer their ownership shares.
- **Dissolution.** This section explains the circumstances in which the LLC may be dissolved.

An operating agreement is an internal document, and therefore one does not need to file it with the state. However, it should be updated every time there is a change in membership or management at the company. We recommend reading some samples of operating agreements (which can be easily found for free online) to find the best fit for your company.

Step Six: Get an EIN

As the last step, you will need to get an Employer Identification Number, or EIN, from the IRS. Also known as a Federal Tax Identification Number, your EIN is like a social security number for your LLC.

An EIN is how the IRS tracks your business for tax purposes, but it is also necessary to open a business banking account and legally hire employees.

The good news is that EINs are free and can quickly be obtained by visiting the IRS.gov website.

To recap, these are the six steps to setting up an LLC on your own:

One: Choose your state

Two: Choose a name

Three: Nominate a registered agent

Four: File your articles of organization

Five Create an Operating Agreement

Six: Get an EIN

Congratulations!

Now that you have read and understood how to form an LLC, you might realize that you don't want to do it all by yourself. Fair enough. In that case, you might want to keep reading to understand how to best outsource the LLC creation process.

Hiring a Professional Service

The second way to form an LLC is nearly identical to the first, the only difference being that you pay a company to do for you all the steps mentioned above. There are many professional formation services for hire.

Service packages can involve many aspects of business formation, including drafting operating agreements, so you will have to choose based on your needs and budget.

The most important service that a professional offers, in addition to filing your articles of organization, is acting as your registered agent. This is the service that you most likely should consider using, even if you are filing all your paperwork yourself. Registered agent services typically have a fee ranging from 50 to 150 dollars. This is a small price to pay for the convenience and benefits provided by a professional service.

A hired registered agent helps you stay well-organized. In fact, it will keep your business mail separate and is available at all regular business hours to accept legal papers and official mail on your LLC's behalf. As we have already discussed above, an important additional benefit of using a registered professional agent is privacy. A professional service will provide a level of privacy by withholding your personal name and home address from the LLC's contact information.

There are many reasons you might not want your personal information easily accessible and associated with your business, and hiring a registered professional agent is an easy way to accomplish this.

Now that you have seen the different ways you can form an LLC take some time to research your options. Remember that every state has different laws and that many professional services are available to help you along the way.

Steps You Must Take After You Form an LLC

After you have registered your company as an LLC, you have to ensure that you handle everything properly. You want to make sure that your business is protected moving forward. In this chapter, we are going to go over all the things you need to do once you start your LLC to make sure your business runs smoothly.

Imagine you have just formed your LLC, and you are wondering what you have to do next. There are a number of things that you still need to take care of. The first two steps were already included in the previous chapter, but we give a little refresher.

Operating Agreement

We talked about this in detail in the previous chapter. While technically not mandatory in many states, we included drafting an operating agreement in the steps to take when forming an LLC. Having an operating agreement in place is, in fact, vital to make sure that if anything ever happens with your business, such as getting involved in a lawsuit, you have evidence that you are following the proper procedures.

For instance, if one of your clients is trying to sue you, their attorney may use the lack of an operating agreement as evidence that, although the LLC has been formed, you are not actually operating as an LLC. This could put your personal assets at risk. Therefore, it is highly recommended to draft an operating agreement either during the formation of the LLCor immediately after.

Taxpayer Identification Number

Here is another step that we consider an integrating part of forming an LLC: Obtaining your EIN (Employer Identification Number). An EIN is essential since, without it, you cannot open a bank account for your business and start charging for your products or services.

Bank Account(s)

Once you have obtained your EIN, you need to open a bank account for the LLC. If, until now, you have been operating as a sole proprietorship and you are switching to an LLC, you must make sure that you transfer all the funds from your personal business account into the LLC bank account. Maintaining a clear separation between your personal bank account and your LLC bank account is fundamental.

Depending on the needs of your business, you might want to open up multiple bank accounts. Advantages of having multiple accounts include better security, better tracking of your business' cash flow, and the ability to draft a more accurate budget. Obviously, these pros must be weighed against the additional expenses of opening and maintaining several accounts.

Personal Business License

In case operating your business requires a personal business license or a permit, you would have to apply or reapply after forming your LLC. The license would be for you personally as an owner. For instance, if you want to form an LLC for your attorney business, you are required to have a privileged license from the licensing board in your state.

Vendor Contracts

You need to ensure that you have your contracts in place for your vendors, your clients, or any other business partners. If you switch from a sole proprietorship to LLC and you are still working with the same clients, you can simply change the business owner name in the contract to that of your LLC. It is important that when you sign those contracts, you have a legitimate signature.

When a member signs as a representative of the LLC, he or she should include language clarifying this.

Otherwise (e.g., by simply signing with your name), you may invoke personal responsibility in corporate matters. A standardized signature block can help you avoid this type of confusion.

For instance, if Jane Doe signs on behalf of an LLC, she should clearly indicate that she is signing as a representative of the registered company and her relationship to the LLC. Here is what her signature on behalf of the LLC could look like:

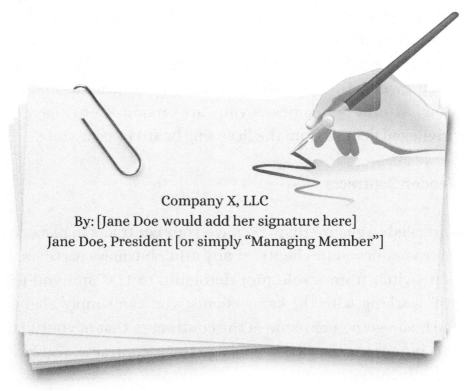

Company X, LLC
By: [Jane Doe would add her signature here]
Jane Doe, President [or simply "Managing Member"]

Always remember to thoroughly read any document that you sign on behalf of the LLC, checking for sentences that could open you up to personal liability.

In case you already have contracts in place with vendors and clients, you must make sure to amend the old contracts with the new signature of the LLC.

Financing, Conversion, Dissolution

How to Fund an LLC

Before we start talking about how to fund your LLC, we must first clarify what it means to be a member of an LLC.

A member of an LLC is also known as an owner. Sometimes entrepreneurs contribute money to an LLC in order to acquire a share in the ownership of the company. However, it is important to note that you can be an owner of an LLCwithout actually investing any funds into it. In fact, you can contribute a service and still become a member (owner).

The bottom line is that you do not necessarily need to contribute capital to become an owner of an LLC. This is yet another instance of the extreme flexibility of LLCs: There are no rigid requirements to be an owner or member of an LLCexcept for being 18 years of age or older.

What is a capital contribution to your LLC?

A capital contribution is an amount that a member of an LLC allocates to the company itself to cover its initial expenses. These may include website design costs, personnel costs for the marketing and accounting team, renting an office, and so on.

The amount and type of such contributions can vary. While the majority of capital contributions are done in cash, a member can also make an initial capital contribution in the form of non-cash assets such as buildings and equipment.

After you have set up your LLC and the founding members have made their personal contributions to cover the initial expenses, you have three main ways of raising additional capital:

- **Equity contribution.** These are funds that are provided in exchange for a stake in the company. Anyone who makes an equity investment into an LLC becomes a member and has rights to the profits or losses of the company. These investments are the most attractive option to business owners since they provide funding that does not need to be repaid. Moreover, equity investments might bring into the company new members that are competent and motivated to make it succeed.

- **Debt investment.** This is money coming from investors who lend money to the LLC with the expectation that the loan will be paid back with interest. This is the most common form of capital for newly formed businesses. However, the company must back up these loans with some collateral. Therefore, a lack of collateral usually limits the amount of capital that can be acquired in this way.

- **Convertible debt.** This is just a combination of the previous two options. When the LLC takes on convertible debt, the company accepts a loan while agreeing to either pay back the money or convert the debt into equity at some time in the future.

It is important to remember that every person who buys equity into the company becomes a member and can participate in any type of member resolution that requires some form of voting. The new member must comply with a set of obligations and responsibilities that are outlined in the LLC operating agreement. Once again, we see how important it is for the operating agreement to be specific in describing each member's contributions, their percentage of ownership, as well as any sort of profit allocation. It should also be established in the agreement what happens if one of the members decides to leave the LLC.

Conversion: S Corp to LLC

An S Corp (S Corporation) is a corporate structure authorized by the Internal Revenue Code to transfer taxable income, credits, deductions, and losses directly to shareholders. The S Corp is a viable option only for small businesses with 100 or fewer shareholders and is similar in many respects to the limited liability company (LLC).

Both S Corps and LLCs are known as "pass-through entities" for tax purposes. Therefore, any income deductions or tax credits are passed through to the business owners and, thus, filed on those owners' individual tax returns. There is no corporate tax return that must be filed for an LLC or S-corp. For this reason, these two types of business structures avoid the issue of double taxation. In contrast, C corporations are subject to double taxation. The first taxation happens at the corporate level. Then, if the company passes on profit to its shareholders in the form of dividends, the shareholders must also report those dividends on their personal tax returns.

When should you convert from an S corp to an LLC?

As we have just seen, neither of these structures is taxed at the federal level. However, S corps are taxed on certain types of passive income. Since LLCs benefit from fewer formalities, simplified operations, and more flexible tax options, you may find it convenient to turn your S corp into an LLC.

For most types of businesses, LLCs are the best structure due to their simplicity, while adding a corporate status might needlessly complicate things. If you're not planning to sell stocks, or seek angel investor funding or venture capital, then you are probably better off as an LLC. An S corp structure, on the other hand, may be better for large, complex companies.

One of the first things you should be mindful of is that there are tax consequences for converting an S Corp to an LLC. It is important that you are aware of such tax implications, as they can heavily affect your business.

To successfully convert your company to an LLC, you will probably have to liquidate your S corp. For tax purposes, it is as if the corporation sold all of its assets. If the corp's assets have increased between the time of the formation of the business and the time of its conversion to an LLC, then capital gain is realized. Hence the shareholders will have to pay capital gains tax on the amount of that gain.

All this considered, it may still be appropriate to convert your business structure. Especially in the following circumstances:

The S-corp wants to create a liability shield. In most states, LLC members are shielded from creditors by what is called charging order statutes. Under a charging order, a creditor of the LLC can legally withhold money from distributions operated by the company until the debt is extinguished.

However, a charging order does not provide the creditor with management rights in the LLC, nor can the creditor intervene in the running of the enterprise to which the debtor is a member. In most states, a charging order is the only way for the creditor of an LLC to recoup the money owed to them. Only in some states, the creditor can be authorized by the court to force the liquidation of the business to satisfy their claim against the debtor.

The S corp needs to liquidate assets ahead of time. We have seen that the S corp must liquidate assets if it is to be converted to an LLC. This could also be viewed as a benefit to a company that continues to grow exponentially. An S Corp that is experiencing massive and rapid growth might want to convert while the tax consequences of such liquidation are lower than at a later point. In fact, taxes would continue to increase based on the value of the assets to liquidate.

The S corp wants to bring in an inadmissible investor. It could be investor number 101 or a foreign citizen who is not a US resident. In these cases adding such "inadmissible" investors would cause the immediate termination of the S corporation. Transitioning to an LLC might be an appropriate way to bring in these investors.

In conclusion, choosing whether or not to convert an S-Corp to an LLC depends on your specific situation. Keep in mind that an LLC is one of the simplest business entities and structures to operate and manage.

Based on your type of business, the number of members, and whether you have investors or not, you should evaluate if it is appropriate to convert your S Corp into an LLC.

Conversion: Sole Proprietorship to LLC

Many new entrepreneurs start out their businesses as sole proprietors. That is, they run a one-person enterprise in which there is no legal distinction between the owner and the business entity. To gain more financial control over their business as well as liability protection, they may wish at some point to transition from a Sole Proprietorship to an LLC.

If you have been operating a business as a sole proprietorship and you decide that, for liability reasons or tax purposes, you want to transition to an LLC, there is good news for you. In fact, the process that you will have to go through is not that different from just normally forming an LLC with a new business.

First, you need to create an LLC. You can read more about the concrete steps you must take in the chapter of this book titled "How to Form an LLC." The main step is filing a document with your state's Secretary of State. Once you file the Articles of Organization or Certificate of Formation (the names of the documents vary from state to state) and they are approved, your LLC is formed.

Here are the additional points to consider when converting a sole proprietorship to an LLC.

The business name. If your sole proprietorship was operating under a trade name or a DBA and you want to continue operating under that DBA ("doing business as") with your LLC, then you will need to withdraw the current trade name registration and refile it with your LLC. If the name of the LLC is the same as your sole proprietorship's DBA, however, you don't need to worry about refiling the trade name. In this case, you will just operate under your LLC's name.

The EIN. Remember that one of the steps to undertake as soon as you have formed an LLC is to get an EIN (tax identification number) through the IRS. You may have had an EIN for your sole proprietorship if it had employees or if your bank required it, but now that you are changing to an LLC, it is mandatory that you get a new EIN since the LLC is a brand new entity. After getting the new EIN, you will have to update your bank account information so that it has the LLC's name and new tax ID number.

Permits and licenses. If your sole proprietorship was required to have any sort of permit or license to operate, you want to inquire whether you are required to add the name of your LLC on those documents.

Contracts. When converting from a sole proprietorship to an LLC, all the contracts must be amended to include the name of the newly formed LLC.

Dissolution

Dissolving an LLC simply means closing or shutting down your business. What are some of the most common reasons why business owners choose to dissolve their LLCs? The first one is to avoid paying the annual state renewal fees when they are no longer conducting business. The payment of these recurring fees keeps the LLC active. Even if your LLC stops operating, the state will continue to charge annual fees, and it may even add interest if they are not paid on time. The state will not let you officially dissolve the LLC until all outstanding taxes and fees have been paid in full. To avoid paying late fees, penalties, and interest fees, as well as to protect yourself from potential liabilities, it is important to officially dissolve your LLC the right way and in accordance with your state's requirements.

Ultimately, there is no need to be alarmed if your LLC has been inactive, but be sure not to wait too long to dissolve it.

How do you properly dissolve your LLC?

Generally, dissolving your business just involves filing a form to the business division of your state's secretary of state.

The state may also require that you pay the state fee and send payments along with the dissolution documents. In some states, there is no charge, and in others, the fee can be hundreds of dollars. It is important to check with the business division at your secretary of state's office to find out the exact procedure.

Once you have taken the decision to dissolve your company, there are several steps to undertake to move things along, including notifying creditors, filing final tax returns, and informing all relevant government agencies. Here we summarize the most important points.

1. Vote to Dissolve the LLC

When members decide to dissolve the company, they take part in what is called voluntary dissolution. This can happen after they have cast a vote or because they are following the company's guidelines for events that automatically trigger dissolution, such as the death of a member. Refer to your LLC's operating agreement for proper procedures. In case your operating agreement does not address dissolution, you should follow the procedures described in your state's LLC laws.

After every member has voted and a majority agrees (or a cause for dissolution has occurred), make a record of this decision to dissolve the LLC and store it in the company's official records.

2. File Your Final Tax Return

In some states, you will have to obtain a tax clearance or good standing verification from the state tax agency before you can file the dissolution paperwork. Filing the final tax return and paying any taxes that are still due will satisfy this requirement. When you file the tax return for the company, be sure to indicate somewhere that this will be its last tax return. You will then receive authorization in the form of a certificate or letter from the IRS stating that you no longer have tax obligations.

Even if your state does not require a tax clearance, you still have to file your final tax return at both the state and federal levels, as well as the final employment tax return. Failing to do so might make you personally liable for unpaid payroll taxes.

3. File an Article of Dissolution

An article of dissolution is a document in which you ask the state to officially dissolve your LLC.

You can find the form at your state's corporate division or on the Secretary of State's website. The form generally requires you to provide information about the company and its members and details about the company's assets and liabilities.

Once your article of dissolution has been approved and you have paid any processing fees, the state will send you a certificate of dissolution. Keep this important document in your files.

4. Settle Outstanding Debts

Even if your state might not require you to notify creditors before filing the dissolution deed, it is a good idea to do it anyway. In this way, you can pay all your company's obligations and reduce the possibility of unexpected claims arising in the future.

Creditors may include lenders, insurers, service providers, and suppliers. The notice should tell them a deadline for filing claims advising them that claims filed after the deadline will be barred. The appropriate deadline is set by your state's law, but it is usually between 90 and 180 days.

5. Distribute Assets

After you have paid your company's creditors as well as any outstanding taxes, all the remaining assets (including investments, profits, and tangible assets) can be distributed to the LLC owners. The operating agreement (or state law, if you do not have one) will set the terms of such distribution.

6. Conduct Wind Down Processes

Properly winding up the business includes several steps, such as firing employees, paying payroll taxes, canceling contracts, leases, business licenses, and permits, as well as notifying customers of the last date of business.

At the end of this process, you must close the company's bank accounts, federal employer identification number (FEIN), and state tax identification number, in case you have one.

In conclusion, if you are no longer using your LLC, then it is important to dissolve it. In this way, you can avoid getting hit with fees and potential interest payments. Be wary that some states will not let you officially dissolve the LLC until you pay everything that is owed to them.

How to Pay Yourself as an LLC

As the owner of an LLC, there are several different ways in which you can pay yourself.

Single-Member LLC

As a single-member LLC, the payment method is also known as the draw of the owner. Remember that the IRS considers single-member LLCs to be "disregarded entities." This means that the owner and business are one and the same thing when it comes to taxes. To be specific, your LLC profits will be treated as personal income instead of business income.

When you own a single-member LLC, you do not only use your Social Security Number for identification purposes. In addition, you are also identified with the EIN. You can apply for an EIN as soon as you form an LLC. It is mandatory to have one so that you can open up your business account. To avoid liability, you should be strict in separating your personal account from your business bank account.

When you transfer money from your business bank account to your personal account, you are taking a so-called distribution. You have simply distributed money to yourself. The company is passing business profits on to its owner.

This process is straightforward for a single-member LLC, but it can be more complex if you're part of a multi-member LLC. In that case, one needs to consider the operating agreement to understand how profits are allocated and at what frequency.

The main advantage of this system of distribution to pay yourself is its simplicity. However, the drawback is that you'll pay FICA, Medicare, and Social Security taxes (commonly called "self-employment tax") on all the revenue of your business instead of on only a fixed salary.

As a single-member LLC, your business does not receive a tax deduction when it writes you a check. This is because you are not processing payroll with a payroll company. When you pay your employees, you receive a deduction, but when you pay yourself, you receive no deduction.

One solution is to pay yourself as an employee. If you restrict yourself to what the IRS considers "reasonable compensation," then you can choose to be treated as an S-corporation for your taxes.

If you elect NOT to be treated as a corporation for tax purposes, then you are not restricted to a conventional salary. As the owner of a single-member LLC, you can pay yourself through distribution, also known as an "owner's draw." How much money and how often you draw is up to you, but ideally, you should leave sufficient funds in the corporate account to operate and grow the business.

Multi-Member LLC

Members of a multi-member LLC also use the owner's draw method to pay themselves. Each member can draw as many or as few shares as he or she wishes, as long as this complies with the company's operating agreement and sufficient funds remain for the daily costs and performance of the company.

If there are enough fund reserves, these LLCs can establish guaranteed payments for members. Analogous to salaries, guaranteed payments are paid regardless of the results of the business.

Corporate LLCs

Salaries and distributions

In case an LLC has chosen to be treated as an S corporation or a C corporation for tax purposes, its members (also called shareholders) are not allowed to take owner's draws.

67

Instead, they are considered employees. Therefore, they must pay themselves a fixed salary on the company's regular payroll, with taxes deducted. This can be done using payroll software or by outsourcing the work to professionals.

As an LLC owner, you can determine the amount of your salary, but that amount must meet the requirements of "reasonable compensation." This is defined by the IRS as "the value that would normally be paid for similar services by similar businesses under similar circumstances."

In addition to your salary, you can also pay yourself distributions or dividends, which are distributions that come from a company's profit. Remember that distributions and dividends are considered taxable income.

Common LLC Mistakes You Can Easily Avoid

Although limited liability companies offer protection to the business owner, and many entrepreneurs form an LLC to shield their personal assets from confiscation in the case of a lawsuit, there are instances when your personal assets are at risk.

What are the risks?

Piercing the veil

What is piercing the veil?

Veil piercing is a means by which courts ignore the separate existence of the LLC. Since the entity is no longer there, the business owner becomes liable for the debts of the company.

Breaking the veil can be an issue for companies regardless of how big they are. However, the most common case is for a corporation or LLC with one or a few owners when it is not capable of paying its debt.

Usually, the creditor sues the corporation or LLC for the outstanding payment. Once that happens, the LLC has to pay off the debt. If that still does not happen, the creditor ends up suing the business owners and asks the court to "pierce the veil" to hold the business owners personally liable.

To ensure the best possible protection for your personal assets, you should avoid these common mistakes made by LLC owners:

Not writing an operating agreement

We have already discussed the details contained in the operating agreement. For instance, how the LLC is run, plans to buy a property or other assets for the company, how you and the other members are paid, what start-up investments you and the other member will contribute to the enterprise, what type of business activity the company is engaged in, potential insurance, licenses, and permits that are required to run the business, where the business is located, and finally what happens in case the company is dissolved.

It is crucial that you include in the operating agreement any relevant information that defines the business. This can appear an overwhelming task, as there are a lot of details. However, an operating agreement helps identify your business as an entity separate from yourself in case of a lawsuit.

A detailed and professionally compiled operating agreement adds a further layer of protection, making it unlikely that your personal affairs get mixed up with your business affairs.

Not recording meeting minutes

This step is not strictly required for LLCs. However, we strongly recommend you record minutes every time a meeting is held. You should aim to conduct a meeting with all the members at least once every year. Carefully record the place, date, and time where the meeting took place. Write down any change in the membership structure or in the business model and major investments or acquisitions in which the company has been involved during that year. Keep these notes (the so-called meeting minutes) in a folder together with all the important documents related to your LLC.

Even if your company is a Single-Member LLC, you can still write meeting minutes. If this is your situation, it will be more of an annual report in which you discuss the evolution of your business during the last 12 months. Once again, having a collection of reports of this kind is useful to establish that the company is being run properly as an entity separate from you as an individual.

No bookkeeping

The third most common mistake of LLC owners is not doing proper bookkeeping. It is fundamental to track and keep a record of any expense or revenue generated by the LLC. If you do that, you will have a much easier time when you have to file your taxes. Make sure your bookkeeping is also timely. Do not postpone the recording of revenues or expenses but go ahead and do it as soon as possible. This will lower the risk of forgetting to record some transactions. Clear and transparent bookkeeping records will help you justify your balances in case of a tax audit. An online service such as Quickbooks can be extremely helpful in tracking your monthly revenue and expenses.

Not having a business account

As we have seen before, one of the first steps you should take after forming your LLC is opening a bank account for your business. This is necessary if you want to keep your finances and those of your business separate.

If you don't have a separate account for your business, it will be easier to pierce the corporate veil when you are involved in litigation. Remember that to open a business bank account, you need your EIN number.

Not financing your LLC properly

If you operate too many transactions between the LLC's account and your personal bank account, then the corporate veil will become easier to pierce during litigation. Make sure at all times that the company's account has enough money to handle a few months of operating expenses. In this way, you will avoid having to constantly transfer money into it from your personal account. This may seem a common sense action, but the truth is that many new LLC owners have the tendency to withdraw money from the company's account as soon as it is deposited.

Signing contracts with your own name

Avoid signing rental contracts or any other type of contract with your name instead of the name of the LLC. For instance, if you are leasing new office space, write the LLC as the entity to which the space is being rented and then sign the documents with your personal signature as the owner of the LLC.

Confusing personal funds and business funds

The only transactions between your personal bank account and that of the LLC should involve funding your business and paying yourself.

Not having any liability insurance

Having some sort of insurance is always recommended since it adds further protection to your personal and company assets. In case of a lawsuit, the insurance company will cover the amount established in your insurance policy.

The alter ego doctrine

The protection and shielding offered by the LLC are not all-encompassing. In court, the following question will be raised. "Is the LLC just an alter ego of its owner, or is it a truly separate entity?" If you make any of the mistakes described above, then the LLC might be regarded as your alter ego during litigation. The court will declare an "alter ego" case if the LLC lacks a separate identity.

Establishing the presence of an alter ego enables the court to pierce the veil and therefore hold the owners personally responsible for the company's debts.

THE ALTER EGO DOCTRINE

Recap: Common mistakes you should avoid when setting up your LLC

1. Not writing an operating agreement

2. Not recording meeting minutes

3. No bookkeeping

4. Not having a business account

5. Not financing your LLC properly

6. Signing contracts with your own name

7. Confusing personal funds and business funds

8. Not having any liability insurance

The bottom line is that you should aim to create the highest degree of separation between you and your company. Keep in mind that abiding by the formalities normally reserved for corporations adds more layers of protection between the LLCand your personal assets.

LLC Glossary

Annual Report — A document that needs to be filed every year. It provides information, such as past performance, financial condition, or business objectives of the limited liability company.

Articles of Organization — The name of the document that needs to be filed in some states to form a limited liability company.

Certificate of Good Standing — A certificate, also called certificate of existence, that serves as evidence for the existence of a limited liability company. It is typically issued by a state official. The certificate authorizes the company to conduct business.

Conversion — Changing your current business structure to a new business structure (e.g., Conversion of an S corp to an LLC).

Corporation — A large company or family of companies created and authorized to act as a single entity.

Dissolution — Dissolving an LLC simply means closing or shutting down its business. By dissolving your LLC, you ensure that you no longer have to pay your annual LLC fees and business taxes or file annual reports.

Distribution — The transfer of money of property by a limited liability company to a member.

Domestic LLC - An LLC is domestic in the state where it is created and foreign everywhere else.

Employer Identification Number (EIN) — A means of identification from the Internal Revenue Service (IRS). Also known as a Federal Tax Identification Number, your EIN is like a social security number for your LLC. An EIN is how the IRS tracks your business for tax purposes, but it is also necessary to open a business banking account and legally hire employees.

Foreign LLC — Despite the name, it does not mean that the company comes from another country. Instead, it means your business was organized under the laws of a different state.

Holding Company — A holding company, or umbrella company, is a parent business entity, that is, a corporation with subsidiaries. These subsidiaries are separate businesses that are wholly or partially owned by the parent.

Liability Insurance — An insurance that helps protect your company in case of a lawsuit. It may protect from various liability claims (e.g., employee injury, damage to the property of others).

Limited Liability Company — An entity incorporated under the Limited Liability Company law of a state. It is a hybrid business structure that contains both characteristics of a corporation and of a partnership.

Managers — The individuals selected by the LLC members to be in charge of the daily operations of an LLC.

Meeting Minutes — A written record of all the votes, discussions, and steps that occurred during an LLC meeting.

Members — The owners of a limited liability company.

Multi-member LLC — An MMLLC has multiple owners. These can be individuals, other LLCs, or corporations. Although technically, an MMLLC can have an arbitrary number of members, the most popular type is a two-member LLCfor businesses run by a husband/wife couple or by two friends who act as partners.

Operating Agreement — The document that provides the basic rules for the conduct of the business and partnerships of the limited liability company. It also contains information on the relationship between business owners and managers.

Signature LLC — The signature of an LLC is different from that of a sole proprietorship in that it clearly defines the line of responsibility. Therefore, the first line of the signature should contain the name of the LLC, followed by the role (e.g., acting president, business owner, manager) and the name of the particular person whose role was previously mentioned.

Single-Member LLC — A single-member limited liability company has only one owner or member. That individual bears the full responsibility of the company, including being accountable for tax payments.

Sole Proprietorship — An unincorporated business that has only one business owner.

Voting Rights — Members' rights to be involved in the affairs of the company. According to their own interest, they make decisions on all issues that pertain to the business.

LLC FAQ

What documents do I need to file to form an LLC?

When you form an LLC, you need to file various legal documents. The following documents are required to register your company as an LLC:

- Name Reservation Application —As the name says, the Name Reservation Application is used to reserve a name for your LLC. Keep in mind that some states may have restrictions regarding the permissibility of a name and that the chosen name must be available.

- Articles of Organization — It must be filed through the Secretary of State. You can download the form from the website of the Secretary of State.

- An operating agreement —It contains regulations related to how the business should be run. It includes the rights of the members and information on relationships between managers and members of the organization.

Note: Depending on your location, you may not be required to file all of the above-mentioned documents.

Who is liable for LLC debt?

The liable entity for an LLC's debt is the LLC itself. Creditors can only go after the assets held by the LLC unless one of the LLC's members personally co-signed a business loan, put up their own property as collateral, committed fraud, or if the LLC's corporate veil has been pierced.

The corporate veil is the phrase used to describe the limited liability protection that forming an LLC gives its owners.

When you form an LLC, your personal assets, such as your house or your car, will not be on the line if your business is sued. Nevertheless, the corporate veil has its limits.

LLC owners need to take steps to make sure that their corporate veil does not get pierced. For instance, they need to ensure that they do not mix their business and personal finances, have enough capital to cover their liabilities, sign business documents on behalf of the LLC, document company affairs, or maintain the LLC's good standing with the state.

What happens if my LLC is inactive?

Due to illness, I abandoned my LLC a few years back. I am sure I received requests from the state, but I bravely ignored them. I am a little more nervous now - how should I address this, if at all? I did nothing with it, and I made no income.

Many states will dissolve LLCs after a certain period of time if the LLC does not remain compliant (i.e., they fail to file an annual report). LLCs that fail to file their annual report with the state may lose their good standing and may end up dissolved or forfeited.

If you want to revive an LLC, you will have to contact the state for the reinstatement package. If your LLC has remained compliant, it will remain active until you file a certificate of dissolution.

Can an LLC have an unlimited life?

Thanks to recent changes to the IRS tax code, LLCs can now be created without setting a dissolution date, therefore allowing them to have potentially unlimited life.

What is the difference between "Managers" and "Members" in an LLC?

Members of an LLC are similar to stockholders of corporations. In fact, a synonym for "members" is "owners." They own a piece of the company based on the value of their initial investment.

Managers, instead, are people chosen by the members to coordinate, run, and manage the day-to-day operations of the company. A manager may or may not be a member of the LLC.

Is an LLC required to hold meetings?

One of the main advantages of an LLC is that it has fewer formal requirements than a corporation. One of them is having regular meetings.

When forming an LLC, you can state in your operating agreement whether you want to hold meetings and with which frequency. Not requiring meetings results in less paperwork and, therefore, a lower risk of not complying with the law.

How much is the cost of forming and operating an LLC?

In certain states, you may be required to pay an annual fee when you file your annual report. In addition, depending on your location, you may have to pay state taxes.

In some states, you will be subject to annual fees for your LLC. Here are some examples of states and the LLC costs that you would incur in those states:

California

In California, you would have to pay a $20 reporting fee. This payment must be made as soon as you file an LLC, as well as every two years afterward (i.e., as long as your LLC is still operating). Furthermore, you would have to pay an $800 LLC tax. This tax fee is due every year on the 15th day of the fourth month that the LLC was registered. Keep in mind that this is a recurring annual fee. If your LLC's income is higher than $250,000, it may owe further state tax.

Nevada

In Nevada, you must pay a $150 fee for the Initial List of Members and Managers. In addition, you would have to pay a $200 fee for Business license registration and renewals.

The Business license application fee must be paid within the first month of filing the LLC. No state taxes must be paid in Nevada.

Delaware

The only fee that LLCs must pay in Delaware is an annual fee of $300. It has to be paid each year on June 1 after the LLC has been formed.

New York

In New York, it is mandatory to have publications of news about the LLC in two newspapers in the county where the LLC is registered. Publication fees can be as high as $2000. As soon as the publication is done, the company must pay a $50 filing fee and submit to the state a certificate of publication.

What are some differences between an S-Corporation and an LLC?

S-corporations and LLCs are very similar, but there are a few important differences. An LLC has fewer restrictions and more flexibility in the running of its operation. Some of the restrictions of an S-corporation are being limited to one class of stock and not being permitted more than 100 stockholders.

There are also important differences between the two business structures when it comes to taxes. Owners of an LLC are required to pay self-employment taxes on all of their profits, while S-corporation shareholders do not have to pay taxes on anything above their annual salary (as long as this is considered by the IRS to be "reasonable compensation"). Remember that an LLC can also elect to be treated as an S corp for tax purposes (see the chapter "How to pay yourself as an LLC").

When I file articles of organization or amendment, how many copies do I need to send?

Only one. Send two copies only if the filer wants a copy bearing the filing stamp.